THOUGHTS
ON BIRDS

By

WILLIAM WORDSWORTH

Copyright © 2020 Ragged Hand

This edition is published by Ragged Hand,
an imprint of Read & Co.

This book is copyright and may not be
reproduced or copied in any way without the
express permission of the publisher in writing.

British Library Cataloguing-in-Publication Data
A catalogue record for this book is available
from the British Library.

Read & Co. is part of Read Books Ltd.
For more information visit
www.readandcobooks.co.uk

CONTENTS

William Wordsworth 5
THE GREEN LINNET. 11
TO A SKY-LARK, 1807. 13
TO A SKYLARK, 1827. 15
TO THE CUCKOO. 16
THE SPARROW'S NEST. 18
A WREN'S NEST. 19
ANIMAL TRANQUILLITY AND DECAY.
A SKETCH. 23
RESOLUTION AND INDEPENDENCE. 24
THE CONTRAST — THE PARROT
AND THE WREN. 31
SUGGESTED BY A PICTURE OF THE
BIRD OF PARADISE. 34
POOR ROBIN. 36
TO A REDBREAST — IN SICKNESS. 38
THE REDBREAST. 39
THE REDBREAST AND THE BUTTERFLY. 43
HARK! 'TIS THE THRUSH,
UNDAUNTED, UNDEPREST. 45
THE DUNOLLY EAGLE. 46

EAGLES..47

BIBLIOGRAPHY................................48

William Wordsworth

"Mr. Wordsworth . . . had a dignified manner, with a deep and roughish but not unpleasing voice, and an exalted mode of speaking.

He had a habit of keeping his left hand in the bosom of his waistcoat; and in this attitude, except when he turned round to take one of the subjects of his criticism from the shelves (for his contemporaries were there also), he sat dealing forth his eloquent but hardly catholic judgments. . . . Walter Scott said that the eyes of Burns were the finest he ever saw. I cannot say the same of Mr. Wordsworth; that is, not in the sense of the beautiful, or even of the profound. But certainly I never beheld eyes which looked so inspired and supernatural.

They were like fires half burning, half smouldering with a sort of acrid fixture of regard, and seated at the further end of two caverns. One might imagine Ezekiel or Isaiah to have had such eyes.

The finest eyes, in every sense of the word,

which I have ever seen in a man's head (and I have seen many fine ones), are those of Thomas Carlyle."—1815.

An Excerpt from
The Autobiography of Leigh Hunt, 1850

"His features were large, and not suddenly expressive; they conveyed little idea of the 'poetic fire' usually associated with brilliant imagination. His eyes were mild and up-looking, his mouth coarse rather than refined, his forehead high rather than broad; but every action seemed considerate, and every look self-possessed, while his voice, low in tone, had that persuasive eloquence which invariably 'moves men.'"—1832.

An Excerpt from
Memories of Great Men. . . , 1871
by Anna Maria Hall

". . . He (Wordsworth) talked well in his way; with veracity, easy brevity, and force, as a wise tradesman would of his tools and workshop,—

and as no unwise one could. His voice was good, frank, and sonorous, though practically clear, distinct, and forcible, rather than melodious; the tone of him business-like, sedately confident; no discourtesy, yet no anxiety about being courteous.

A fine wholesome rusticity, fresh as his mountain breezes, sat well on the stalwart veteran, and on all he said and did. You would have said he was a usually taciturn man; glad to unlock himself to audience sympathetic and intelligent when such offered itself.

His face bore marks of much, not always peaceful, meditation; the look of it not bland or benevolent so much as close, impregnable, and hard: a man *multa tacere loquive paratus*, in a world where he had experienced no lack of contradictions as he strode along! The eyes were not very brilliant, but they had a quiet clearness; there was enough of brow, and well-shaped; rather too much of cheek ('horse face' I have heard satirists say); face of squarish shape, and decidedly longish, as I think the head itself was (its 'length' going horizontal); he was large-boned, lean, but still firm-knit, tall, and strong-looking when he stood, a right good old steel-gray figure, with rustic simplicity and dignity about him, and a vivacious strength looking through him which might have suited one of those old steel-gray markgrafs whom Henry the Fowler set up to ward the 'marches' and do battle with the heathen in a stalwart and judicious manner."

An Excerpt from
Reminiscences, 1881
by Thomas Carlyle.

BIRD POETRY

BY
WILLIAM WORDSWORTH

THE GREEN LINNET.

Beneath these fruit-tree boughs that shed
Their snow-white blossoms on my head,
With brightest sunshine round me spread
Of spring's unclouded weather,
In this sequestered nook how sweet
To sit upon my orchard-seat!
And birds and flowers once more to greet,
My last year's friends together.

One have I marked, the happiest guest
In all this covert of the blest:
Hail to Thee, far above the rest
In joy of voice and pinion!
Thou, Linnet! in thy green array,
Presiding Spirit here to-day,
Dost lead the revels of the May;
And this is thy dominion.

While birds, and butterflies, and flowers,
Make all one band of paramours,

Thou, ranging up and down the bowers,
Art sole in thy employment:
A Life, a Presence like the Air,
Scattering thy gladness without care,
Too blest with any one to pair;
Thyself thy own enjoyment.

Amid yon tuft of hazel trees,
That twinkle to the gusty breeze,
Behold him perched in ecstasies,
Yet seeming still to hover;
There! where the flutter of his wings
Upon his back and body flings
Shadows and sunny glimmerings,
That cover him all over.

My dazzled sight he oft deceives,
A brother of the dancing leaves;
Then flits, and from the cottage-eaves
Pours forth his song in gushes;
As if by that exulting strain
He mocked and treated with disdain
The voiceless Form he chose to feign,
While fluttering in the bushes.

TO A SKY-LARK, 1807.

Up with me! up with me into the clouds!
   For thy song, Lark, is strong;
Up with me, up with me into the clouds!
   Singing, singing
With all the heavens about thee ringing,
   Lift me, guide me till I find
That spot which seems so to thy mind!

I have walked through wildernesses dreary,
   And to-day my heart is weary;
   Had I now the wings of a Faery,
   Up to thee would I fly.
There is madness about thee, and joy divine
   In that song of thine;
Up with me, up with me, high and high,
To thy banqueting-place in the sky!
   Joyous as Morning,
   Thou art laughing and scorning;
Thou hast a nest, for thy love and thy rest:
And, though little troubled with sloth,

Drunken Lark! thou would'st be loth
To be such a Traveller as I.
    Happy, happy Liver!
With a soul as strong as a mountain River,
Pouring out praise to the Almighty Giver,
    Joy and jollity be with us both!
    Hearing thee, or else some other,
    As merry a Brother,
I on the earth will go plodding on,
By myself, cheerfully, till the day is done.

TO A SKYLARK, 1827.

Ethereal minstrel! pilgrim of the sky!
Dost thou despise the earth where cares abound?
Or, while the wings aspire, are heart and eye
Both with thy nest upon the dewy ground?
Thy nest which thou canst drop into at will,
Those quivering wings composed, that music still!

Leave to the nightingale her shady wood;
A privacy of glorious light is thine;
Whence thou dost pour upon the world a flood
Of harmony, with instinct more divine;
Type of the wise who soar, but never roam;
True to the kindred points of Heaven and Home!

TO THE CUCKOO.

O blithe New-comer! I have heard,
I hear thee and rejoice.
O Cuckoo! shall I call thee Bird,
Or but a wandering Voice?

While I am lying on the grass
Thy twofold shout I hear;
From hill to hill it seems to pass,
At once far off, and near.

Though babbling only to the Vale
Of sunshine and of flowers,
Thou bringest unto me a tale
Of visionary hours.

Thrice welcome, darling of the Spring!
Even yet thou art to me
No bird, but an invisible thing,
A voice, a mystery;

The same whom in my school-boy days
I listened to; that Cry
Which made me look a thousand ways
In bush, and tree, and sky.

To seek thee did I often rove
Through woods and on the green;
And thou wert still a hope, a love;
Still longed for, never seen.

And I can listen to thee yet;
Can lie upon the plain
And listen, till I do beget
That golden time again.

O blessèd Bird! the earth we pace
Again appears to be
An unsubstantial, faery place;
That is fit home for Thee!

THE SPARROW'S NEST.

BEHOLD, within the leafy shade,
Those bright blue eggs together laid!
On me the chance-discovered sight
Gleamed like a vision of delight.
I started—seeming to espy
The home and sheltered bed,
The Sparrow's dwelling, which, hard by
My Father' house, in wet or dry
My sister Emmeline and I together visited.

She looked at it and seemed to fear it;
Dreading, tho' wishing, to be near it:
Such heart was in her, being then
A little Prattler among men.
The Blessing of my later year
Was with me when a boy:
She gave me eyes, she gave me ears;
And humble care, and delicate fears;
A heart, the fountain of sweet tears;
And love, and thought, and joy.

A WREN'S NEST.

Among the dwellings framed by birds
In field or forest with nice care,
Is none that with the little Wren's
In snugness may compare.

No door the tenement requires,
And seldom needs a laboured roof;
Yet is it to the fiercest sun
Impervious, and storm-proof.

So warm, so beautiful withal,
In perfect fitness for its aim,
That to the Kind by special grace
Their instinct surely came.

And when for their abodes they seek
An opportune recess,
The hermit has no finer eye
For shadowy quietness.

These find, 'mid ivied abbey-walls,
A canopy in some still nook;
Others are pent-housed by a brae
That overhangs a brook.

There to the brooding bird her mate
Warbles by fits his low clear song;
And by the busy streamlet both
Are sung to all day long.

Or in sequestered lanes they build,
Where, till the flitting bird's return,
Her eggs within the nest repose,
Like relics in an urn.

But still, where general choice is good,
There is a better and a best;
And, among fairest objects, some
Are fairer than the rest;

This, one of those small builders proved
In a green covert, where, from out
The forehead of a pollard oak,
The leafy antlers sprout;

For She who planned the mossy lodge,
Mistrusting her evasive skill,
Had to a Primrose looked for aid
Her wishes to fulfill.

High on the trunk's projecting brow,
And fixed an infant's span above
The budding flowers, peeped forth the nest
The prettiest of the grove!

The treasure proudly did I show
To some whose minds without disdain
Can turn to little things; but once
Looked up for it in vain:

'Tis gone—-a ruthless spoiler's prey,
Who heeds not beauty, love, or song,
'Tis gone! (so seemed it) and we grieved
Indignant at the wrong.

Just three days after, passing by
In clearer light the moss-built cell
I saw, espied its shaded mouth;
And felt that all was well.

The Primrose for a veil had spread
The largest of her upright leaves;
And thus, for purposes benign,
A simple flower deceives.

Concealed from friends who might disturb
Thy quiet with no ill intent,
Secure from evil eyes and hands
On barbarous plunder bent,

Rest, Mother-bird! and when thy young
Take flight, and thou art free to roam,
When withered is the guardian Flower,
And empty thy late home,

Think how ye prospered, thou and thine,
Amid the unviolated grove
Housed near the growing Primrose-tuft
In foresight, or in love.

ANIMAL TRANQUILLITY AND DECAY.

A SKETCH.

The little hedgerow birds,
That peck along the road, regard him not.
He travels on, and in his face, his step,
His gait, is one expression; every limb,
His look and bending figure, all bespeak
A man who does not move with pain, but moves
With thought. -He is insensibly subdued
To settled quiet: he is one by whom
All effort seems forgotten; one to whom
Long patience hath such mild composure given
That patience now doth seem a thing of which
He hath no need. He is by nature led
To peace so perfect, that the young behold
With envy what the Old Man hardly feels.

RESOLUTION
AND INDEPENDENCE.

There was a roaring in the wind all night;
The rain came heavily and fell in floods;
But now the sun is rising calm and bright;
The birds are singing in the distant woods;
Over his own sweet voice the Stock-dove broods;
The Jay makes answer as the Magpie chatters;
And all the air is filled with pleasant noise of waters.

All things that love the sun are out of doors;
The sky rejoices in the morning's birth;
The grass is bright with rain-drops;—on the moors
The hare is running races in her mirth;
And with her feet she from the plashy earth
Raises a mist, that, glittering in the sun,
Runs with her all the way, wherever she doth run.

I was a Traveller then upon the moor;
I saw the hare that raced about with joy;
I heard the woods and distant waters roar;

Or heard them not, as happy as a boy:
The pleasant season did my heart employ:
My old remembrances went from me wholly;
And all the ways of men, so vain and melancholy.

But, as it sometimes chanceth, from the might
Of joys in minds that can no further go,
As high as we have mounted in delight
In our dejection do we sink as low;
To me that morning did it happen so;
And fears and fancies thick upon me came;
Dim sadness—and blind thoughts, I
   knew not, nor could name.

I heard the sky-lark warbling in the sky;
And I bethought me of the playful hare:
Even such a happy Child of earth am I;
Even as these blissful creatures do I fare;
Far from the world I walk, and from all care;
But there may come another day to me—
Solitude, pain of heart, distress, and poverty.

My whole life I have lived in pleasant thought,
As if life's business were a summer mood;

As if all needful things would come unsought
To genial faith, still rich in genial good;
But how can He expect that others should
Build for him, sow for him, and at his call
Love him, who for himself will take no heed at all?

I thought of Chatterton, the marvellous Boy,
The sleepless Soul that perished in his pride;
Of Him who walked in glory and in joy
Following his plough, along the mountain-side:
By our own spirits are we deified:
We Poets in our youth begin in gladness;
But thereof come in the end despondency and madness

Now, whether it were by peculiar grace,
A leading from above, a something given,
Yet it befell that, in this lonely place,
When I with these untoward thoughts had striven,
Beside a pool bare to the eye of heaven
I saw a Man before me unawares:
The oldest man he seemed that ever wore grey hairs.

As a huge stone is sometimes seen to lie
Couched on the bald top of an eminence;

Wonder to all who do the same espy,
By what means it could thither come, and whence;
So that it seems a thing endued with sense:
Like a sea-beast crawled forth, that on a shelf
Of rock or sand reposeth, there to sun itself;

Such seemed this Man, not all alive nor dead,
Nor all asleep—in his extreme old age:
His body was bent double, feet and head
Coming together in life's pilgrimage;
As if some dire constraint of pain, or rage
Of sickness felt by him in times long past,
A more than human weight upon his frame had cast.

Himself he propped, limbs, body, and pale face,
Upon a long grey staff of shaven wood:
And, still as I drew near with gentle pace,
Upon the margin of that moorish flood
Motionless as a cloud the old Man stood,
That heareth not the loud winds when they call,
And moveth all together, if it move at all.

At length, himself unsettling, he the pond
Stirred with his staff, and fixedly did look

Upon the muddy water, which he conned,
As if he had been reading in a book:
And now a stranger's privilege I took;
And, drawing to his side, to him did say,
"This morning gives us promise of a glorious day."

A gentle answer did the old Man make,
In courteous speech which forth he slowly drew:
And him with further words I thus bespake,
"What occupation do you there pursue?
This is a lonesome place for one like you."
Ere he replied, a flash of mild surprise
Broke from the sable orbs of his yet-vivid eyes.

His words came feebly, from a feeble chest,
But each in solemn order followed each,
With something of a lofty utterance drest—
Choice word and measured phrase, above the reach
Of ordinary men; a stately speech;
Such as grave Livers do in Scotland use,
Religious men, who give to God and man their dues.

He told, that to these waters he had come
To gather leeches, being old and poor:

Employment hazardous and wearisome!
And he had many hardships to endure:
From pond to pond he roamed, from moor to moor;
Housing, with God's good help, by choice or chance;
And in this way he gained an honest maintenance.

The old Man still stood talking by my side;
But now his voice to me was like a stream
Scarce heard; nor word from word could I divide;
And the whole body of the Man did seem
Like one whom I had met with in a dream;
Or like a man from some far region sent,
To give me human strength, by apt admonishment.

My former thoughts returned: the fear that kills;
And hope that is unwilling to be fed;
Cold, pain, and labour, and all fleshly ills;
And mighty Poets in their misery dead.
—Perplexed, and longing to be comforted,
My question eagerly did I renew,
"How is it that you live, and what is it you do?"

He with a smile did then his words repeat;
And said that, gathering leeches, far and wide

He travelled; stirring thus about his feet
The waters of the pools where they abide.
"Once I could meet with them on every side;
But they have dwindled long by slow decay;
Yet still I persevere, and find them where I may."

While he was talking thus, the lonely place,
The old Man's shape, and speech—all troubled me:
In my mind's eye I seemed to see him pace
About the weary moors continually,
Wandering about alone and silently.
While I these thoughts within myself pursued,
He, having made a pause,
   the same discourse renewed.

And soon with this he other matter blended,
Cheerfully uttered, with demeanour kind,
But stately in the main; and, when he ended,
I could have laughed myself to scorn to find
In that decrepit Man so firm a mind.
"God," said I, "be my help and stay secure;
I'll think of the Leech-gatherer on the lonely moor!"

THE CONTRAST —
THE PARROT AND THE WREN.

I

Within her gilded cage confined,
I saw a dazzling Belle,
A Parrot of that famous kind
Whose name is Non-Pareil.

Like beads of glossy jet her eyes;
And, smoothed by Nature's skill,
With pearl or gleaming agate vies
Her finely-curved bill.

Her plumy mantle's living hues
In mass opposed to mass,
Outshine the splendour that imbues
The robes of pictured glass.

And, sooth to say, an apter Mate
Did never tempt the choice

Of feathered Thing most delicate
In figure and in voice.

But, exiled from Australian bowers,
And singleness her lot,
She trills her song with tutored powers,
Or mocks each casual note.

No more of pity for regrets
With which she may have striven!
Now but in wantonness she frets,
Or spite, if cause be given;

Arch, volatile, a sportive bird
By social glee inspired;
Ambitious to be seen or heard,
And pleased to be admired!

II

This moss-lined shed, green, soft, and dry,
Harbours a self-contented Wren,
Not shunning man's abode, though shy,
Almost as thought itself, of human ken.

Strange places, coverts unendeared,
She never tried; the very nest
In which this Child of Spring was reared,
Is warmed, thro' winter, by her feathery breast.

To the bleak winds she sometimes gives
A slender unexpected strain;
Proof that the hermitess still lives,
Though she appear not, and be sought in vain.

Say, Dora! tell me, by yon placid moon,
If called to choose between the favoured pair,
Which would you be, the bird of the saloon
By lady-fingers tended with nice care,
Caressed, applauded, upon dainties fed,
Or Nature's darkling of this mossy shed?

SUGGESTED BY A PICTURE OF THE BIRD OF PARADISE.

The gentlest Poet, with free thoughts endowed,
And a true master of the glowing strain,
Might scan the narrow province with disdain
That to the Painter's skill is here allowed.
This, this the Bird of Paradise! disclaim
The daring thought, forget the name;
This the Sun's Bird, whom Glendoveers might own
As no unworthy Partner in their flight
Through seas of ether, where the ruffling sway
Of nether air's rude billows is unknown;
Whom Sylphs, if e'er for casual pastime they
Through India's spicy regions wing their way,
Might bow to as their Lord. What character,
O sovereign Nature! I appeal to thee,
Of all thy feathered progeny
Is so unearthly, and what shape so fair?
So richly decked in variegated down,
Green, sable, shining yellow, shadowy brown,
Tints softly with each other blended,

Hues doubtfully begun and ended;
Or intershooting, and to sight
Lost and recovered, as the rays of light
Glance on the conscious plumes touched here and there?
Full surely, when with such proud gifts of life
Began the pencil's strife,
O'erweening Art was caught as in a snare.

A sense of seemingly presumptuous wrong
Gave the first impulse to the Poet's song;
But, of his scorn repenting soon, he drew
A juster judgment from a calmer view;
And, with a spirit freed from discontent,
Thankfully took an effort that was meant
Not with God's bounty, Nature's love to vie,
Or made with hope to please that inward eye
Which ever strives in vain itself to satisfy,
But to recall the truth by some faint trace
Of power ethereal and celestial grace,
That in the living Creature find on earth a place.

POOR ROBIN.

Now when the primrose makes a splendid show,
And lilies face the March-winds in full blow,
And humbler growths as moved with one desire
Put on, to welcome spring, their best attire,
Poor Robin is yet flowerless; but how gay
With his red stalks upon this sunny day!
And, as his tufts of leaves he spreads, content
With a hard bed and scanty nourishment,
Mixed with the green, some shine not lacking power
To rival summer's brightest scarlet flower;
And flowers they well might seem to passers-by
If looked at only with a careless eye;
Flowers — or a richer produce (did it suit
The season) sprinklings of ripe strawberry fruit.

But while a thousand pleasures come unsought,
Why fix upon his wealth or want a thought?
Is the string touched in prelude to a lay
Of pretty fancies that would round him play
When all the world acknowledged elfin sway?

Or does it suit our humour to commend
Poor Robin as a sure and crafty friend,
Whose practice teaches, spite of names to show
Bright colours whether they deceive or no? —
Nay, we would simply praise the free good-will
With which, though slighted, he, on naked hill
Or in warm valley, seeks his part to fill;
Cheerful alike if bare of flowers as now,
Or when his tiny gems shall deck his brow:
Yet more, we wish that men by men despised,
    And such as lift their foreheads overprized,
Should sometimes think, where'er they chance to spy
This child of Nature's own humility,
What recompence is kept in store or left
For all that seem neglected or bereft;
With what nice care equivalents are given,
How just, how bountiful, the hand of Heaven.

TO A REDBREAST — IN SICKNESS.

Stay, little cheerful Robin! stay,
And at my casement sing,
Though it should prove a farewell lay
And this our parting spring.

Though I, alas! may ne'er enjoy
The promise in thy song;
A charm, 'that' thought can not destroy,
Doth to thy strain belong.

Methinks that in my dying hour
Thy song would still be dear,
And with a more than earthly power
My passing Spirit cheer.

Then, little Bird, this boon confer,
Come, and my requiem sing,
Nor fail to be the harbinger
Of everlasting Spring.

THE REDBREAST.

Driven in by Autumn's sharpening air
From half-stripped woods and pastures bare,
Brisk Robin seeks a kindlier home:
Not like a beggar is he come,
But enters as a looked-for guest,
Confiding in his ruddy breast,
As if it were a natural shield
Charged with a blazon on the field,
Due to that good and pious deed
Of which we in the Ballad read.
But pensive fancies putting by,
And wild-wood sorrows, speedily
He plays the expert ventriloquist;
And, caught by glimpses now—now missed,
Puzzles the listener with a doubt
If the soft voice he throws about
Comes from within doors or without!
Was ever such a sweet confusion,
Sustained by delicate illusion?
He's at your elbow—to your feeling

The notes are from the floor or ceiling;
And there's a riddle to be guessed,
'Till you have marked his heaving chest,
And busy throat whose sink and swell,
 Betray the Elf that loves to dwell
In Robin's bosom, as a chosen cell.

Heart-pleased we smile upon the Bird
If seen, and with like pleasure stirred
Commend him, when he's only heard.
But small and fugitive our gain
Compared with hers who long hath lain,
With languid limbs and patient head
Reposing on a lone sick-bed;
Where now, she daily hears a strain
That cheats her of too busy cares,
Eases her pain, and helps her prayers.
And who but this dear Bird beguiled
The fever of that pale-faced Child;
Now cooling, with his passing wing,
Her forehead, like a breeze of Spring:
Recalling now, with descant soft
Shed round her pillow from aloft,
Sweet thoughts of angels hovering nigh,

And the invisible sympathy
Of "Matthew, Mark, and Luke, and John,
Blessing the bed she lies upon?"
 And sometimes, just as listening ends
In slumber, with the cadence blends
A dream of that low-warbled hymn
Which old folk, fondly pleased to trim
Lamps of faith, now burning dim,
Say that the Cherubs carved in stone,
When clouds gave way at dead of night
And the ancient church was filled with light,
 Used to sing in heavenly tone,
Above and round the sacred places
They guard, with winged baby-faces.
Thrice happy Creature! in all lands
Nurtured by hospitable hands:
Free entrance to this cot has he,
Entrance and exit both yet free;
And, when the keen unruffled weather
That thus brings man and bird together,
Shall with its pleasantness be past,
And casement closed and door made fast,
To keep at bay the howling blast,
He needs not fear the season's rage,

For the whole house is Robin's cage.
Whether the bird flit here or there,
O'er table lilt, or perch on chair,
Though some may frown and make a stir,
To scare him as a trespasser,
And he belike will flinch or start,
Good friends he has to take his part;
One chiefly, who with voice and look
Pleads for him from the chimney-nook,
Where sits the Dame, and wears away
Her long and vacant holiday;
With images about her heart,
Reflected from the years gone by,
On human nature's second infancy.

THE REDBREAST
AND THE BUTTERFLY.

Art thou the Bird whom Man loves best,
The pious Bird with the scarlet breast,
   Our little English Robin;
The Bird that comes about our doors
When Autumn winds are sobbing?
Art thou the Peter of Norway Boors?
   Their Thomas in Finland,
   And Russia far inland?
The Bird, whom by some name or other
All men who know thee call their Brother,
The Darling of Children and men?
Could Father Adam open his eyes,
And see this sight beneath the skies,
He'd wish to close them again.

If the Butterfly knew but his friend,
Hither his flight he would bend;
   And find his way to me
Under the branches of the tree:

In and out, he darts about;
Can this be the Bird, to man so good,
That, after their bewildering,
Did cover with leaves the little children,
   So painfully in the wood?

What ailed thee, Robin, that thou could'st pursue
   A beautiful Creature,
That is gentle by nature?
Beneath the summer sky
From flower to flower let him fly;
'Tis all that he wishes to do.
The Cheerer Thou of our in-door sadness,
He is the Friend of our summer gladness:
What hinders, then, that ye should be
Playmates in the sunny weather,
And fly about in the air together!
His beautiful wings in crimson are drest,
A crimson as bright as thine own:
If thou would'st be happy in thy nest,
O pious Bird! whom Man loves best,
Love him, or leave him alone!

HARK! 'TIS THE THRUSH, UNDAUNTED, UNDEPREST.

Hark! 'tis the Thrush, undaunted, undeprest,
By twilight premature of cloud and rain;
Nor does that roaring wind deaden his strain
Who carols thinking of his Love and nest,
And seems, as more incited, still more blest.
Thanks; thou hast snapped a fireside Prisoner's chain,
Exulting Warbler! eased a fretted brain,
And in a moment charmed my cares to rest.
Yes, I will forth, bold Bird! and front the blast,
That we may sing together, if thou wilt,
So loud, so clear, my Partner through life's day,
Mute in her nest love-chosen, if not love-built
Like thine, shall gladden, as in seasons past,
Thrilled by loose snatches of the social Lay.

THE DUNOLLY EAGLE.

Not to the clouds, not to the cliff, he flew;
But when a storm, on sea or mountain bred,
Came and delivered him, alone he sped
Into the castle-dungeon's darkest mew.
Now, near his master's house in open view
He dwells, and hears indignant tempests howl,
Kenneled and chained. Ye tame domestic fowl,
Beware of him! Thou, saucy cockatoo,
Look to thy plumage and thy life! The roe,
Fleet as the west wind, is for 'him' no quarry;
Balanced in ether he will never tarry,
Eyeing the sea's blue depths. Poor Bird! even so
Doth man of brother man a creature make
That clings to slavery for its own sad sake.

EAGLES.

Composed at Dunollie Castle in the Bay of Oban.

Dishonoured Rock and Ruin! that, by law
Tyrannic, keep the Bird of Jove embarred
Like a lone criminal whose life is spared.
Vexed is he, and screams loud. The last I saw
Was on the wing; stooping, he struck with awe
Man, bird, and beast; then, with a consort paired,
From a bold headland, their loved aery's guard,
Flew high above Atlantic waves, to draw
Light from the fountain of the setting sun.
Such was this Prisoner once; and, when his plumes
The sea-blast ruffles as the storm comes on,
Then, for a moment, he, in spirit, resumes
His rank 'mong freeborn creatures that live free,
His power, his beauty, and his majesty.

BIBLIOGRAPHY

THE GREEN LINNET
   Composed in 1803, First published in *Poems, in Two Volumes, Volume II*, 1807.

TO A SKY-LARK, 1807
   Composed in 1805 and first published in *Poems, in Two Volumes, Volume I,* 1807

TO A SKY-LARK, 1827
   Composed in 1825, first published in 1827. Published in *The Poetical Works of William Wordsworth, Volume VII*, 1896. One of the *Poems of the Imagination*.

TO THE CUCKOO
   Composed in 1802. First published in *Poems, in Two Volumes, Volume II*, 1807. One of the *Poems of the Imagination*.

THE SPARROW'S NEST
   Composed in 1801 and first published in *Poems, in two Volumes, Volume II*, 1807.

A WREN'S NEST

Composed in 1833 and first published in *Memorials of the Tour*, 1835. Included as one of the *Poems of the Fancy* Series.

ANIMAL TRANQUILLITY AND DECAY

Composed in 1798 and first published in *Lyrical Ballads, First Edition*, 1798. In the edition of 1798, the poem was called, *Old Man Travelling; Animal Tranquillity and Decay, a Sketch*. In 1800, the title was *Animal Tranquillity and Decay. A Sketch*. In 1845, it was *Animal Tranquillity and Decay*. It is included among the *Poems Referring to the Period of Old Age*.

RESOLUTION AND INDEPENDENCE

Begun in May, finished in July, 1802. First published in *Poems, in Two Volumes, Volume I*, 1807.

THE CONTRAST – THE PARROT AND THE WREN

Composed in 1825 and first published in 1827. Published in *The Poetical Works of William Wordsworth, Volume VII*, 1896. One of the *Poems of the Fancy*.

SUGGESTED BY A PICTURE OF THE BIRD OF PARADISE

First published in 1842, One of the *Poems of the Imagination*. Published in *The Poetical Works of William Wordsworth, Volume VII*, 1896.

POOR ROBIN

Composed in March 1840 and first published in 1842. Published in T*he Poetical Works of William Wordsworth, Volume VIII*, 1896.

TO A REDBREAST - IN SICKNESS

First published in 1842. Published in *The Poetical Works of William Wordsworth, Volume VIII*, 1896.

THE REDBREAST

First published in *Yarrow Revisited, and Other Poems*, 1835.

THE REDBREAST AND THE BUTTERFLY

Composed in April, 1802. First published in *Poems, in two Volumes, Volume I*, 1807. Included among the *Poems of the Fancy*.

"HARK! 'TIS THE THRUSH, UNDAUNTED, UNDEPREST"

First published in 1838. One of the *Miscellaneous Sonnets*. Published in *The Poetical Works of William Wordsworth, Volume VIII*.

THE DUNOLLY EAGLE

First published in *Poems composed or suggested during a Tour in the Summer of 1833*, 1833.

EAGLES

First published in *Yarrow Revisited, and Other Poems*, 1835.

Printed in Great Britain
by Amazon